—Marley, 6

I wish God could take out all the bad people, or just make them believe.

-A'leah, 13

I want God to wear a bird T-shirt.

-Adrian, 3

I wish God could
give me the power of time.

-Joshuah, 11

I wish God could draw
a picture of my
whole family.
-Giulia, 5

I wish God would
give me a sister.
-Sophia, 6

I wish God could give radioactive powers!

-Brandon, 8

WHat Do YOU WiSH GOD COULD Do?

(When a mother's hug and 911 aren't enough.)

Help everyone
in need.
-Carter, 6¾

I wish that God could
save people's lives and let them
live forever. I wish that he
could help get the bad guy from
hurting other people on earth.
-Dillon, 9

Heal the sick.
-Lorelei, 7

I wish I could fly.
Can I? Or do only birds
get to do that?
-Caleb, 7

I wish that he could create more animals and nature. I wish he could create more babies. I wish he could create a new invention instead of the stuff in the world. I wish he could create magic like fairy magic.

—Brooke, 6

I wish that God could heal me when my stomach hurts. He already does everything . . . pretty much.

—Kyla, 12

I wish he could stop people from being poor.

—Maddi, 8

I wish God could stop wars and give every child who is less fortunate a real house, and clean clothing, and a loving family.

—Olivia, 11

I wish God would
stop all the wars and stop
people being poorly.
—Jacob, 8

I wish he was real.
—Daphne, 6

I wish God could fix
Sophie and bring my grama back.
—Layla, 8

I wish that he could bring
people back who are dead, and I
wish he can make a wish you had
come true as soon as God heard you.
And that there's no wars—that
he can stop all wars.
—Maude Rose, 9

I wish God could swim!
And fly.
  -Piper, 5

I wish God can
turn me into a wolf.
  -Iva, 9

I wish God could
make it snow chocolate
and rain chocolate milk
or mango juice.
  -Arie, 8¾

Make peace and
enlighten me on decisions
I wonder about.
  -Katrina, 10

Help me with
everyday things.
  -Saskia, 8

Hmmm. I wish he
could make more Nerf guns.
  -James, 8

I wish God could make me famous—soon!
-Kaela, 8¾

I wish God had a phone so that I could talk to him, 'cause I don't know if he hears me when I'm praying.
-Eve, 8

I wish God could make no one die except all the bad people.
-Mia, 11

I wish God could do magic.
-Liam, 5

I wish God could make me invisible.
-Hugh, 8

I wish God could convince my mom and dad to give me Wii, lego batman and, lego starwars like the ones my friend has.

-Isaac, 5

I want God to touch
a shark's mouth.
-Anthony, 4

I wish God would make
everything out of Popsicles:
Popsicle rain
and Popsicle storms.
-Isabella, 7

I want God to
make peace, because
God can do anything.
-Jacob, 7

I wish God would give me
a Lego ninja turtle.
-Callum, 5

I wish God
could make me rich!
-Corie, 12

god   loves you

love

I wish God could
give me for my birthday
a 3-D TV.

-William, 10

I wanted to swim in a lake near our house but my mom says it's dead. Could you please make us a new one?

-Brittany, 7

I wish God could change the way I act . . .

-Jazmine, 12

I wish God could keep people safe.

-Xainyia, 7

I wish God could make it so there was no such thing as money so there would be no poor or rich people then there would be no stealing. Everyone could have everything that they needed, and everything would be fair, and nobody would be homeless. I'd also like him to make it so that nobody killed any animals.

-Luke, 8

Hi God:

How are you? I know you do lots of great things for the world. I like that you can make the weather do whatever you want it to. I would like special powers too. I am fine most of the time but sometimes I want to have lots of stuff like my cousins and some of my friends have, like mycousin Gaylen who has every Lego machine ever made and my friend Connor does too. Thank you for listening to me.
From your friend,
Christopher

-Christopher, 9

WHY DO
WE NEED GOD?

(The very idea of God reminds us to be good.)

Because
her build us.
-Vivi, almost 4

Because no one
can just go up to the sky
and create the ground and everything,
so God needs to do it.
-Jordan, 5

So we can live.
-Emily, 5

To give us love,
and then we give it
to each other.
-Annabel, 8

Because he
made the world.
-Evan, 7

I call God when I need
help with things, but not my
homework because my mom says
I have to do that myself.

—Jackson, 7

God is way more
important than the
President.

—Arli, 8

Because God loves everyone,
even the bad people.

—Kendra, 6

God always goes to his
home to do magic and all kinds
of stuff because no one
is stronger than him.

—Liam, 5

So that he
could stop people
from being poor.

—Maddie, 8

God makes winter go away
so that summer can come.
-Dax, 7

God is the person
that you should make
wishes to, not Santa Claus!
-Bradley, 8

God walks me to
school every day so
that I will be protected.
-Rebecca, 6

My mom
talks to God when
we need more money.
-Manny, 6

God rides in my
dad's car so we don't
have accidents.
-Cole, 6

People want a notion
that death isn't the end.
-Eli, 12

Make everyone get
what they deserve and let
world peace happen.

-Anonymous

We need God so that
he can make miracles happen.
He used to make more
in the olden days.

-Kaela, 8¾

Hi God:

My name is Carly and I live in
Prestwick. I have one brother, his
name is Brendon and he is six. He is
my best friend. We have a white rat
called Percy and a dog called Banjo.
Thank you for being around us.

I love you,
Carly

-Carly, 8

WHAT IS GOD'S JOB?

(A very difficult one.)

making the world.
  —Vivi, almost 4

God looks after all
the angels and takes care
of the entire world.
  —Layla, 8

God's job is
always to be awake.
  —Abby, 4

To make the earth—I think a
couple of meteors banged into each
other and then they kept crashing until
a herd of meteors smashed together
till the earth got made.
  —Jonny, 7¾

To let us live.
  —Emily, 5

He made everything in
eight days. So he worked for
seven days and then he rested
in the night on the seventh.
He was, like, very tired.

-Evan, 7

To create the world.

-Jordan, 5

God's job is to
find us if we get lost.

-Max, 8

He made the whole world.
He made people.

-Noah, 5

Well, he actually made two people.
He made Adam and used his ribs to
make Eve. Adam was a boy but
Eve was a girl. They met and got
married and then had a baby.

-Evan, 7

God protects everybody.

-Carter, 6¾

Because no one can just
go up to the sky and create
the ground and everything,
so God needs to do it.

—Jordan, 5

To give us love,
and then we give it
to each other.

—Liam, 5; Annabel, 8

God starts life.

—Jonny, 7¾

I can't answer
that question. Maybe to
teach us to pray?

—Evan, 7

God's job is to
do magical things, like
speak to animals.

—Jacob, 8

God decides where
the good people go and where
the bad people go.

—Benji, 7

He made an island to put things on.
He made it kind of weird. Like half
Jamaica, half Canada, half Calgary, New
York, and Florida. The first island was
made up of all the other countries and
they were called National Aboriginal.
Then they broke up into other islands
and they all got names and National
Aboriginal got a new name: Winnipeg.

-Evan, 7

God is a security guard,
but for the whole world.

-Declan, 6

God's job is the
biggest and the hardest
because he has to be
everywhere, all the time.

-Stephen, 7

To protect
the world.

-Evan, 7

WHAT IN GOD'S NAME ARE THOSE KID'S TALKING ABOUT?

(Worries, wishes, and lots of wonderful ideas.)

Santa is the most powerful
as he comes bearing gifts!
Then the three wise men . . . what
does God bring to the party?

—Kelly, 9; Natalie, 11

How come if you
made all the flowers, why did
you make robbers, too?

—Ethan, 8

If you made us,
who made you? Do you
have your own God?

—Ariane, 11

If nailing Jesus to the cross hurt so much, why didn't they just use glue instead?

-Oskar, 6

God made mummies and daddies but only the daddies are strong, not the mummies, but no one will say that . . .

-Liam, 5

Mom says God is the boss but my dad still says he is!

-Anonymous

Why aren't I Siri?

-Eli, 12

My father never believed
you were real but my mom did,
but then she got sick and now he
prays to you but my mom
doesn't anymore.
—Max, 8

My mother says
you make all the decisions.
Is that true?
—Brittany, 7

When God gets
tired, Santa helps.
—Megan, 10

God should be
an umbrella for all the
good people.
—Deana, 6 .

I believe that god is just a theory of the human mind.

God lives wherever you imagine.

God wears whatever you imagine.

God cannot change the past, present or future.

To believe in god, you need to imagine.

God does anything you can imagine.

God is not male, nor female.

Uma
age 11

This book is for Remy (Ezra),
my son, the moon and the stars. Thank you,
always, for your inspiration and imagination,
and thank you to all the children who opened
their hearts and minds and shared
their thoughts with me.

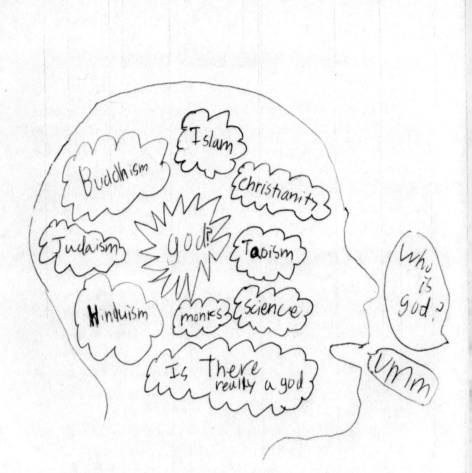

-Emerson, 12

OMG! THE BIG "WHY?"

When our son Remy was born, my husband, a French Canadian Catholic, and I, essentially a mutt born of a High Church of England father and an Austro/Hungarian Jewish mother, knew that we wanted to provide him with a sense of spirituality and godliness, despite our religious differences. To that end, we always told him that God inhabits every living thing including trees, dogs, spiders, and all human beings. We said that although we can't always see God, godliness is always there.

When Remy was seven years old, he told us he knew someone who had really seen God: "When Doctor Sally opened up Grandpa's stomach to get the bad stuff out, God was there, right inside." He then told us that he knew that all doctors see God when they do operations. I was smitten with the imagery. I kept thinking about how he had heard what we said and it had become real for him. I was also thrilled that we were talking about God. That conversation has never stopped.

Over the next several years, I would randomly ask young children how they felt about God. Their answers always surprised and delighted me and, in many cases, made me laugh out loud. On occasion the answers also made me weep. But it wasn't until we entered this new millennium, with our global troubles seeming to escalate at such an alarming rate and in such unimaginable ways, that I began to worry about what the future would hold for the world's children. I know this much: they need to believe in "godliness" now more than ever. I was curious whether they did. I'm happy to report, they do.

The answers I received have educated, illuminated and enchanted me. Looking into a child's mind is akin to opening a treasure chest overflowing with sparkling, unexpected jewels of insight, innocence, and timeless humor. The real surprise came when I began to share the children's wisdom and inventiveness with family and friends. They, in turn, would ask the same questions of their kids and recount their findings back to me. I was excited to learn how much pleasure and inspiration the conversation was generating and so *OMG!* was hatched.

As soon as a child can talk, many parents begin to consider "the God thing" and how best to open the door to religious teachings or just to have that conversation. *OMG!* will, hopefully, help to bring about an understanding that not all faiths view God in the same light, but that doesn't mean that any one faith is wrong—just different. And today, when so many marriages have divergent religious backgrounds, there is a real need for open-ended and open-minded conversations about God. The commitment to providing a spiritual safe harbor has never been more complicated or more necessary as we all try to make sense out of what was once simpler territory; Mr. Rogers' friendly neighborhood has morphed into a much less savory and dangerous terrain where wild things roam. How else do we explain the unspeakable images that flash relentlessly across interminable screens? Now more than ever we need the ultimate comfort zone: the power of GOD.

The notion of God, whether you are a believer or undecided, is so much a part of our reflexive go-to; whether for comfort or for help, as a divining rod when lost, a punching bag when our equilibrium is off kilter, a touchstone, or an inspiration. It just takes one more "o" to remind us that God equals good.

God is always there—familiar and expected much like our daily bread. God is our internal security blanket, with a million and one uses—always welcoming and happy to have us call on him or her, no matter what our need. Simply taking time out, whatever one's circumstance, to speak to God creates the stillness needed to open a personal pathway that helps us find answers to difficult questions without judgment.

Having a spiritual life has been scientifically shown to protect your health. In fact, people who attend religious services live up to fourteen years longer than those who don't. You don't have to go to the church, synagogue, or mosque to experience the health benefits of a rich spiritual life. According to a study done by the University of Colorado, people who are "spiritual but not religious" also experience health benefits; a reduction of stress places less pressure on the nervous system, thereby activating the body's natural self-repair mechanisms, helping the body to heal itself.

With homage to Art Linkletter's, *Kids Say the Darndest Things*, kids do have the most amazing, undiluted candor about everything, and God is no exception. It is my wish that *OMG!* will give you the reassurance that today's kids, just like yesterday's, remain open to hope, and can bring us back to a place of wonder and infinite possibilities. *OMG!* doesn't censor or offer any magical thinking. It's just funny, touching, insightful and spiritually uplifting.

Think of it as a bedside smile before sleeping.

I know God's name! It's Harold. I heard people singing about it. Harold be thy name . . .

—Monica Parker, at age 5

"What do you think of God,"
the teacher asked.
After a pause, the young pupil replied,
"He's not a think, he's a feel."

—Paul Frost

WHO IS GOD?

(That's the question I set out to answer, only to discover
there are so many answers and even more questions.)

God is a spirit.
-Layla, 8; Olivia, 8; Adrian, 3

God is a girl.
-Isabella, 4

God is the King of
the World.
-Kelly, 9

God is the
creator of earth.
-Saskia, 12; Eli, 12

God is either a
woman or a man I'm
not sure which (neather
do you) so I drew
God half woman half
man.

-Mia, 11

God is the creator
of the earth and more.
-Ariane, 11

God, in my eyes, is really awesome.
I want to follow what he did
by helping my community and trying
my hardest at school and things
like that . . . he is everything.
-Kyla, 12

Umm . . .
-Lorelei, 7

A spirit
who cares for us.
-Jacob, 8

He was a little boy and
some people put him on a cross.
He went to heaven and all the
other people went to him.
-Lion, 7

God is the Lord,
the Creator.
-Zoe, 10

God is the guy who
created the world.
-Ari, 8

God is the person who
created the universe.
-Maddi, 8

God is a holy man
that makes planets
and the world.
-Angel, 6

I have no idea.
But gods are good guys.
-Daphne, 6

God is someone who died
a long time ago and he owns heaven
and he's very kind to let
people go there.
-Maude Rose, 9

God is God!
-James, 8

God is my dad.
-Josiah, 7

God is someone that
listens to me, someone
that is always there.
-Katrina, 11

God is like a king
only better.
-Alex, 7

Grandma is God.

-Piper, 5

I think God is a
big hug that goes all
around the world.

-Liam, 5

I believe that God is everything.
He is our ruler, he is our father,
and he is our friend.
-Stephany, 12

God is love.
-Xainyia, 7

God is a really,
really famous spirit.
-Leo, 5

He's a man or a woman.
-Kaela, 8¾

I think God is a myth.
I like myths like unicorns or
dragons, and I like him.
-Jonny 7¾

God is a grownup.
And he absolutely loves people.
He doesn't like people that fight.
Neither does Santa or Jesus!

-Liam, 5

He is a person who looks over us making sure nothing is getting out of hand! However he cannot stop things from happening, but rather he hopes for the best.

-Olivia, 11

God is my best friend.

-Joshuah, 11

God is like an umbrella that protects people from bad things. Like an insurance company.

-Anonymous

-Isaac, 6

BY: Carter

sky
God

God

Us

girl God

boy God

-Carter, 6¾

Dear God:

You are watching us night and day.
When we are sad you make us happy.
When we are happy you make us laugh.
When we are angry you make us cool.
You are watching us—you let us know when
we are doing bad things. You decide when
we are going to die. You decide when we
live. You decide when it is day and you
decide when it is night. You decide who
is bad and who is good. I think you
are nice. The sun and the world are in
your hands. I hope everyone out there
thinks so too.

Love,
Charlotte xoxo :)

-Charlotte, 8

WHAT DOES GOD LOOK LIKE?

(The master of the universe is the master of disguise.)

God is a shadow who
follows us wherever we go.
—Bradley, 8

His hair is like . . .
he's bald I think.
—Maude Rose, 9

God has long white hair
and a white beard and a
white face but he wears blue
clothes and blue shoes.
—Minny, 6

God is so beautiful
you can't see him.
—Rebecca, 6

kaela

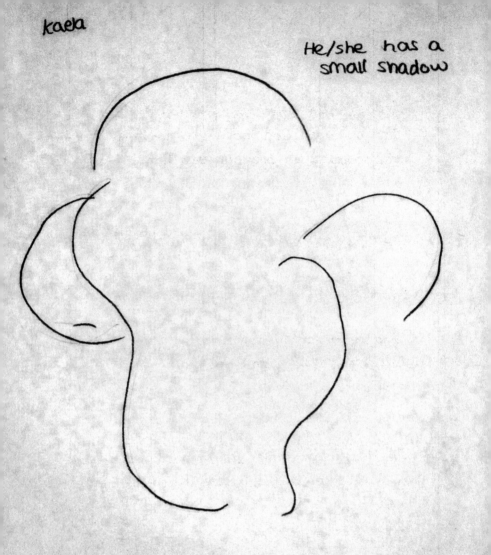

I think god is invisible.

I can't draw a picture of
God because God looks like nothing,
because no one can see him.

-Jordan, 5

God had white hair,
but he dyes it brown.

-Emily, 5

God is powerful and
has muscles that can save
the whole world.

-Liam, 5

It's a big secret
what God looks like,
because he's one of us.

-Cole, 8

Like a cloud
like a genie.

-Lion, 7

Like a statue.

-Vivi, almost 4

MAKALA

GOD

GOD

-Makala, 5

God looks like a
half boy on one side and a
half girl on the other.

-Jonny, 7

Jonny

I can't draw a picture of
God because God looks like nothing,
because no one can see him.
-Jordan, 5

God had white hair,
but he dyes it brown.
-Emily, 5

God is powerful and
has muscles that can save
the whole world.
-Liam, 5

It's a big secret
what God looks like,
because he's one of us.
-Cole, 8

Like a cloud
like a genie.
-Lion, 7

Like a statue.
-Vivi, almost 4

MaKaLa

GOd

GOd

-Makala, 5

God looks like a
half boy on one side and a
half girl on the other.

-Jonny, 7

Jonny

God kind of looks like the wind,
breathing, and whistling.
The wind brings God beside us
sort of like a prayer.

-Liam, 5

God looks like a
leafless sapling.

-Evan, 8

God is a spirit
that looks like a
ball of light.

-Avaya, 6

God needs someone to
take his picture, so we'd know
what he looks like. Maybe he
could do a selfie.

-Abby, 7

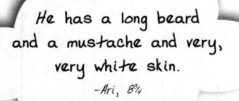

He has a long beard
and a mustache and very,
very white skin.

-Ari, 8¾

God has giant ears
so he can hear everything
we are saying.
-Gabby, 9

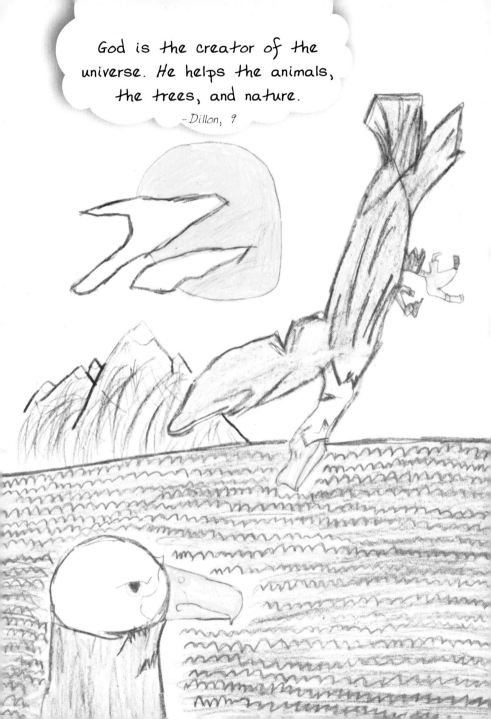

God is the one who created all things. God is the one who made me, the father almighty.

-Brooke, 6

God is a superhero for the world.

-Angel, 5

God's got an invisible
head & he floats in the
garden. One side is night
and the other side is day
and God sees the owls &
bunnies and butterflies.
God also rides a motorcycle
but he's playing hockey in
Pasadena right now.
He can do everything.

-Kamran, 8

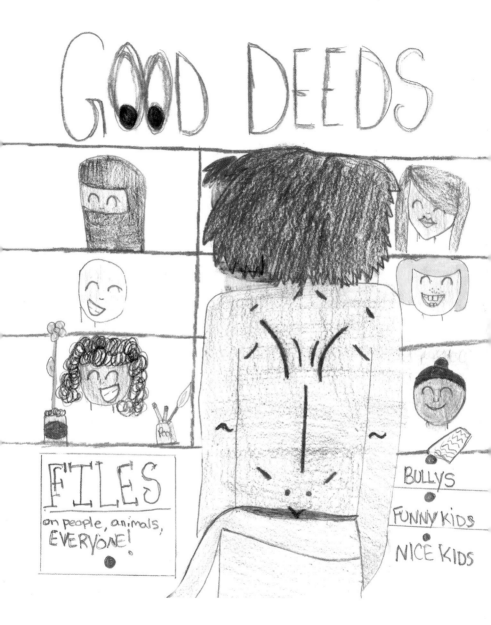

-Olivia, 11

God is magic.
-Layla, 8

WHAT DOES GOD WEAR?

(God's fashion sense is all encompassing, from cloaks to Dino underpants.)

God wears a cloak
that takes away people's sins.
—Dillon, 9

He has a brown robe with
a white belt and he has all the
magic powers in the world.
—Giulia, 5

He is always wearing
a smile on his face unless
someone sins, then he frowns.
He wears a white garment.
—Kyla, 12

God wears a
big white robe with
white and silver
sparkles.

-Natalie, 10

God wears a rainbow robe and sunglasses.

-Jordan, 5

God wears a purple robe with a blue trimming.

-Anonymous

He wears a robe and holds a wand and stick. He wears a robe thing with the arms and a staff beside him. He has a cross necklace that he wears that holds all his magic in it.

-Maude Rose, 9

God wears
a white robe.
-Zackenya 6

God wears an American
flag and shines lots of bright
light down on good people.

-Stephen, 9

God always wears a shiny
dinner plate behind his head
as well as a wrinkled sheet.

-Nick, 9

-Anonymous

God wears nature.
His clothes are made of the
elements of nature—leaves,
sand, stone, and wood.

-Layla, 8

God wears white clothes.

-Ariane, 11

White clothes.
Torn clothes.

-Brooke, 6

He wears free-flowing
white pure clothes.

-Makayla, 11

A white, torn-up robe.

-Celia, 9

God wears a silk toga with jewels and matching shoes, and a golden pendant for good luck, but not for him, for the world.

-Olivia, 11

God is naked.

-Adrian, 3

God wears nothing.

-Piper, 5

God wears nothing because he is invisible.

-Maddi, 8

God wears nothing—he's a spirit.

-Jazmine, 12

God wears silky dresses.
-Daphne, 6, and Birdy, 9

-Birdy, 9

Do you know those white
things that people who are travelling
on camels in the desert wear?
Robes! God wears a white robe.
-James, 8

God wears all white
with sparkles because he is
the highest angel!
-Kelly, 9

God wears rags.
-Jacob, 8

God wears lots
of raggedy, raggedy
clothes.
-Leo, 5

God wears a T-shirt,
a Cubs jumper (sweater),
and trousers.

-Callum, 5

I don't know what
God wears but I think
maybe a cloak.

-Luke, 8

God wears a cloak
because he is old.

-Ari, 8¾

God always wears
white overalls.

-Carter, 6¾

God wears a white suit
with bare feet.

-Anthony, 4

God wears a white dress
but, oh, I've never seen him
but I'll know when I die
at 100 years old.
—Hugh, 8

God wears sandals
and a round coat
with no zipper.
—Liam, 5

God wears a nice
clean robe.
—Corie, 12

God wears a white robe
and Dino underpants.
—Maverick, 5

God wears
a robe of love.
—Xainyua, 7

God wears one side pink
with a skirt and the other
side blue with pants.
—Jonny, 7¾

God wears a robe,
white underwear, golden
colored sandals.
—Joshuah, 11

He wears a blue jacket
and a black wizard hat.
—Lion, 7

God lives
over the rainbow.
-Anonymous

-Gabriel, 5

God lives
in our heart.
-Anonymous

-Catia, 6

In a big church.
-Lion, 7

-Alessandra, 6

WHERE DOES GOD LIVE?

(The Lord's house appears to be far larger than a football field.)

I think that God lives in the temple where he can teach other people and kids about God.

—Dillon, 9

That is a hard one. God lives everywhere.

—Brooke, 6

Everywhere. He is always by my side. He lives in heaven but is always by my side.

—Kyla, 12

God lives everywhere.
    -Mia, 11

God lives in heaven.
    -Jacob, 8; Layla, 8

God lives nearby in Heaven.
    -Leo, 5

God lives in 3rd heaven.
    -Jazmine, 12

God lives in heaven,
which looks like a big ball
of light also.
    -Adrian 4

God lives in heaven
and in me.
    -Xainyia, 7

God lives in the sky, in the heavens, where he has the height to see all of us from above.

—Makayla, 11

God lives up in the sky in heaven watching and protecting us.

—Angel, 6

God lives in heaven, with his son Jesus and in our heart.

—Celia, 10

God lives in our heart but not in our stomachs because then there would be no room for food.

—Anonymous

God lives in heaven
with all the angels to keep
them company.
-Natalie, 10

God lives further than
heaven, in a house with
a bed and everything.
-Jacob, 7

Heaven where God
lives is in outer space.
-Olivia, 8

God lives in his
house in heaven.
-Lion, 7

God lives in his own house
up in the sky. It's called
"The House of the Lord."
-Caleb, 7

He lives in the walls.

-Abby, 4

God lives in a palace in heaven.
He sits beside his son Jesus who
sits on the right side of God.

-Celia, 9

God lives up there!

-Ariane, 11

He lives on a cloud,
in a cloud castle with many
windows so that he can see
everything that's going on.

-Olivia, 11

God lives so high
on a mountain where
there is no green.
-Christie Angel, 8

God lives in your life.
-Piper, 5

He lives up in the sky in heaven.
He lives on a cloud and he has all the
people who have died in the world,
and he gets all those people and
they get to have a happy place.
-Maude Rose, 9

God lives in the sky.
-Maddi, 8; Saskia, 10

Up in the clouds.
-Daphne, 6;
James, 8

Inside God's House.
-Mia, 11

God lives in the sky, in a big cloud in a place called Heaven.

-Liam, 5

God lives with Jesus.

-Vivi, almost 4

God lives at our house.

-Callum, 5

The moon goes in front of the earth and God lives in the back.

-Jonny, 7¾

In a massive land filled with all the dead people that go up to see him.

-Kaela, 8¾

God lives in a light cave
with purple lights all around
him so he can make the
whole cave light.

-Evan, 7

God lives in Olympus,
which is a floating island.

-Carter, 6¾

God lives above and
above space. It's cloudy
and blue and filled with lots
of dead people.

-Ari, 8¾

God lives in a
white house, white everywhere
and white angels.

-Mia, 11

In the wind,
in heaven.

-Liam, 5

On Sundays, God goes home to his family's house to rest.

—Becca, 8

God doesn't have a house. He doesn't need one except on Sundays 'cause that's when he needs to rest.

—Ethan, 8

God has the biggest and best house of everybody, but it's in heaven and it has so much room that all the dead people get to live there too.

—Dana, 8

Dear God:

I know you are everywhere, but I'd like it if you could spend a little more time with me.

Okay?

Bye,

Alex

—Alex, 7

WHERE DOES GOD SLEEP?
DOES GOD SLEEP?

(My guess is, seeing that God is everywhere, he/she is skilled in the art of power naps.)

God doesn't sleep.
His responsibilities are too big.
He has to look after all of us. He has "calm time" instead, where he can be still and quiet but he is still aware.
—Makayla, 11

God does not sleep.
—Brooke, 6

God does NOT sleep.
—James, 8

God sleeps for only one minute.
—Iva, 9

I think that if God sleeps, he sleeps in heaven above all people. But I don't think that God sleeps because he helps people during the nighttime when they get into car accidents and stuff.

-Dillon, 9

God doesn't sleep, except in the crib when he was a baby.

-Isaac, 6

God sleeps up there in his home in his bed.

-Ariane, 11

I don't imagine God sleeping. But I think he does sleep.

-Kyla, 12

He sleeps in your heart.

-Piper, 5

I do not think that God sleeps, but if he did, I think he sleeps in his tomb with silk bed sheets and sheep-fur pillows.
    -Celia, 9

God never sleeps.
He has a place in heaven where he is; it's his home.
    -Layla, 8

Yes. He sleeps in a bed like everyone else but just so that he doesn't miss anything he freezes the world so that he can take a power nap.
    -Olivia, 11

God sleeps on the clouds.
    -Maddi, 8

God sleeps in the clouds.

-Jacob, 8

In the clouds.
But he doesn't sleep.

-Daphne, 6

God has a
special bed that has
a cloud cover.

-Declan, 6

He sleeps on the clouds with his friends,
all the dead people that are good.
I think he regenerates instead of sleeps.
And I think at night he pulls a trigger when
it's night and no one notices it's night.
Then he, like, puts all the dreams
into the kids' heads.

-Maude Rose, 9

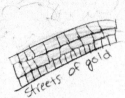
streets of gold

God never sleeps, he
is always watching.
—Jazmine, 12

God sleeps in a heaven
bed, hidden in the clouds.
—Maverick, 5

God doesn't sleep. He stays
up all night to watch the children sleep
all day and all night, and to watch
the grownups to make sure in his mind that
no one has bad dreams. But if someone
has a bad dream, they pray for
God to give them good dreams.
—Liam, 5

God can't sleep ever or everything would be a big mess.
    —Brittany, 7

God sleeps standing with one eye closed at a time.
    —Elena, 9

I don't think God sleeps because he's always watching over the whole world and different countries are awake at different times.
    —Luke, 8

When God is tired he goes to sleep in one of the holes in the moon.
    —Jonny, 7¾

In a bed with a stuffed mini God.
    —Lion, 7

God lives in
the trees.

-Avaya, 6; Adrian, 4

God lives everywhere; he
could be a mountain, a lion,
light, a flower.

-Katrina, 12

God lives in the clouds; heaven....
I think he is so powerful as he is ever-living. I think he has powers that can make him invisible when he wants.
he has loads of fresh fruit
Mia W

-Mia, 11

God's house is way, way back behind a big pearly gate.

-Blair, 10

God lives in paradise
with all of our other committed
companions up in heaven where he
watches and cares over us.

-Stephany, 12

God at his Cloud Desk

M.M
3/29/15
-Makayla, 11

God is a snepard.

God protect us.

God lives in heaven.

God has 7 Billion Friends
(us)

-Simon, 7

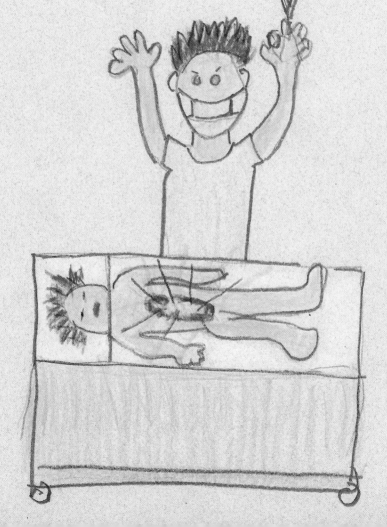

-Maia, 7

-Iva, 9

God just flies
in the sky.

-Isabella, 7

God

God doesn't sleep
because he watches
over us all the time.

-Kelly, 9

God is wearing his
nightshirt to sleep.
-Rick, 8

For sure God has a bed
but it has to be a floating
bed because she floats.
-Isabella, 4

God always looks happy
because he can see all of us.

-Emily, 5

God can do anything!
He is powerful and courageous.
He will always, no matter what,
help you . . . even if you
do not believe in God.

-Kyla, 12

-Zoe, 10

God can do anything!
He is powerful and courageous.
He will always, no matter what,
help you . . . even if you
do not believe in God.

-Kyla, 12

Zoe, 10.

When God gets mad,
he lets out the thunder and
throws lightening around.

-Olivia, 12

Santa is more
powerful than God 'cause
he brings us presents.
-Megan, 8

In my house we have
two gods and they both
give me presents.
-Jess, 6

WHAT CAN GOD DO?

(Miracles, magic, and everything in between.)

Anything.
—Lorelei, 7

God can do anything
he thinks of.
—Jazmine, 12

Everything.
He can move himself
everywhere he wants.
—Evan, 7

God can help us.
—Emily, 5

God is like a Transformer.
He can turn himself into
anything he wants.
—Shane, 7

God can create
anything he has in his mind.
-Corie, 12

God could take me out of
my bed at night to visit my dog,
Cody, who was killed by a
too-fast car.

-Jonathon, 6

God makes the weather.

-Alex, 7

God can give rewards if you are
good and bad things if you are bad.
He keeps a good people book
and a bad people book.

-Mia, 11

God doesn't have a magic wand
but he does magic when he stands
on top of a mountain and waves
his arms at whatever he wants.

-Maggie, 9

He can make people love each other and a lot of other things.

-Isaac, 6

God builds all the planets and makes all the people and the oceans and the light.

-Sophia, 6

God can see everything and everybody in the world and he has special powers.

-Kaela, 8

God can help save people's lives. God can help us through difficult times. He helps us out when there is trouble.

-Dillon, 9

God brings
the babies to earth.
-Jacob, 7

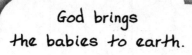

He can
make human beans.
-Jordan, 5

He makes the world
and he makes us.
-Viv, almost 4

What can God do?

God can do many things. Like protect them wen alone.

-Celia, 10

God does many things like
saving lives and he moves the earth
so the sun comes up and down and
with moon. He helps plants grow.

-Celia, 9

Create more things.
Give love to people.
He can do everything!

-Brooke, 6

God can do anything if not everything.
He created the world and everything
around us. I believe it started with
the most basic necessities and we were
influenced by evil to lead to all the
negative in the world. But one day
he will return and make everything right
for those who have faith.

-Stephany, 12

God cures people.
God keeps the life-cycle going.
God makes babies.
God loves people.

—Isaac, 6

He can hope for the best
for the world and try to make it
a better place for everyone.

—Olivia, 11

Change the world.

—Daphne, 6

He makes the trees,
the water, everything!

—James, 8

He's a man that protects
all people and children. And he protects
our land. He can send people down like
he can make wishes come true.
He can make sure people can't get hurt
sometimes. He can also put magic on
people, like when it's night he can put magic
on people who can't sleep so they can sleep.
At night, God puts all the dreams in the
children's heads when they sleep.

-Maude Rose, 9

God eats grapes.

-Iva, 9

God can grow you and he can
dance but he cannot type.

-Piper, 5

God makes life nicer,
a ray of light.

-Katrina, 12

God protects us.
-Anthony, 4

God has all the
magical powers in the world.
He can do anything.
-Giulia, 5

-James, 7

God does magic.
-Jonny, 7¾

God flies all over the sky.
-Isabella, 7

God can make it rain
and make it snow.
-Ari, 8¾

God can do magical
things like speak to animals.
-Jacob, 8

God can grow plants and
vegetables, make sand, and he
gives us eyes and lovely, lovely hair.
God makes us safe.
-Callum, 5

God can create
things in the world, like
clouds and lakes.
-Maddie, 8

-Kayla, 7

God sits at a
big desk in the clouds and
watches us everywhere.
—Jodie, 9

God can eat as much
grapes as he wants, whenever
he would want.
—Carrie, 7

God can bless me.
—Xainyia, 7

God has fun!
—Zackenya, 6

God can turn water
into juice.
—William, 10

God can flood the earth, bless people, kill people, provide for people, heal and save people.
-A'leah, 12

God can do everything, like flying. He could cross the world in two seconds. He could die and come back alive again. He knows everything about us. He knows our future and can do anything he wants with us.
-Luke, 8

God can answer prayers, make miracles and give blessings.
-Jaelynne, 11

He can use his power to save people, he looks after people, and he makes our wishes come true.
-Hugh, 8

IS THERE ANYTHING GOD CANNOT DO?

(It's quite surprising, but apparently God cannot stack boxes.)

Play.
—Lorelei, 7

Well, that is a hard question. God can do anything from heaven but he cannot do stuff right here with us.
—Dillon, 9

Nope . . . well he cannot sin.
—Kyla, 12

God cannot roar. He cannot type.
—Piper, 5

Yeah . . . I mean no . . . he can actually do everything.
—Brooke, 6

God can't change the past but merely help the future along.
—Olivia, 11

God can do everything. There is nothing God can't do.
—Maddie, 8; Layla, 8

God cannot create the earth because scientists discovered something about the Big Bang a few months ago.
—Jacob, 8

God cannot build a house because there are no bricks in heaven.
—Avaya, 6

He cannot bring my daddy back.
—Makayla, 11

god can do everything.

god's house

pearly gate

god

god

-Anonymous

God cannot
stack chairs.
—Adrian, 4

God cannot move the
earth to another place.
—Jonny, 7¾

He cannot stop wars.
He can't stop people from dying
because that's the cycle of life.
If God could, he would try to
save all the people.
—Maude Rose, 9

God cannot
destroy the world.
—Ari, 8¾

God cannot make
me invisible.
—Hugh, 8

God cannot come
into the world and we
can't see him if he did.
—Kaela, 8¾

He cannot be eaten.
He cannot vanish
into thin air.
—James, 8

DOES GOD HAVE FRIENDS?

(God doesn't play favorites. He/she loves everyone.)

Yes —
the dead people.
—Lorelei, 7

Yes, he has a lot of
friends. He loves all people
on earth and in heaven.
—Dillon, 9

Yeah, the three disciples,
Peter, John, and James . . .
plus the whole world.
—Brooke, 6

Yes, everyone is his
friend . . . even if they
do not believe in him.
—Kyla, 12

He has his friends from above and all of us on earth. Our relationship with God is a friendship.

-Makayla, 11

Yes. Goodbye.

-Daphne, 6

God has lots of friends.

-Josiah, 7

God has friends—all the angels and my family.

-Layla, 8

God does not have friends but his children do; his daughters and sons are best friends with Hades, Poseidon, and Zeus' daughters and sons.

-Olivia, 11

All the people in the world that have died are God's friends. He doesn't hurt people, and he doesn't be mean to anyone, and he's never, like, killed anyone.

-Maude Rose, 9

God is friends with all the angels.

-Kaela, 8¾

God is friends with Jesus, and the three kings. They are his cousins.

-Liam, 5

God has a lot of friends but most of them are dead people.

-Anonymous

God is friends with himself.

-Jonny, 7¾

God is friends with
all the angels and all the
people in the sky!
-Jaelynne, 11

God doesn't
have friends because he
is not on earth.
-maddi, 8

All the angels and
people in heaven.
-Natalie, 10

God is friends with all
the people that have died,
like Henry the 8th, Anne Boleyn,
and Queen Elizabeth.
-Anonymous

No. Wait, yes. There are
different types of Gods: one is
god of trees, one of grass, of
water, of fire, and all the
different gods are friends.

-James, 8

God is my friend,
but he's friends with all
the world, even bad people.

-Anonymous

Yes! Mother Nature.

-Piper, 5

I believe that we are all
his friends and children and all those
people above us, accompanying him,
are there to support him and
be his friends forever.

-Stephany, 12

God is friends with all
his workers who are angels.

—Mia, 11

Inside G-d's
house

Maddi   Age 8

.God   is   the   person   who   created   the
university.
God   lives   in   the   sky.
.God   wears   nothing   because   he is   invisible.
.God   sleeps   on   the   clouds.

God   can   create   things   in   the   world, like
Cloud   and   lakes.
I   wish   he   could   stop   people   from   being poor.

God   can   do   everything, There. is   nothing god
Can't - do.
God   doseit have=   Friends   because   he is   not
on   earth.

This   is   god . . . .

I'm killed but powerful.
-Christina, 7

This is God
on the clouds.
-Lorelei, 7

God sees us
whatever we are doing,
wherever we are.

-Gabby, 9

god is watching us

-Sarafina, 11

-Charlotte, 8